Marie McGaha

Marie McGaha

The Root - The Shoot - The Fruit

Marie McGaha

Marie McGaha

Marie McGaha

ISBN-13: 978-0998833958
ISBN-10: 0998833959

Bible verses from the New King James Ver-sion (NKJV)
Spirit Filled Life Bible
Thomas Nelson Publishers ©1991

Marie McGaha

Marie McGaha

Marie McGaha

Marie McGaha

~ One ~
In The Vineyard

"I am the true vine, and My Father is the vinedresser. Every branch in Me that does not bear fruit He takes away; and every branch that bears fruit He prunes, that it may bear more fruit. You are already clean because of the word which I have spoken to you. Abide in Me, and I in you. As the branch cannot bear fruit of itself, unless it abides in the vine, neither can you, unless you abide in Me. I am the vine, you are the branches. He who abides in Me, and I in him, bears much fruit; for without Me you can do nothing. If anyone does not abide in Me, he is cast out as a branch and is withered; and they gather them and throw them into the fire, and they are burned. If you abide in Me, and My words abide in you, you will ask what you desire, and it shall be done for you. By this My Father is glorified, that you bear much fruit; so you will be My disciples."
John 15:1-8
~ * ~

My sitting room is decorated with wall hangings depicting vineyards, grapes, wine, and my favorite has this verse on it. Everything that I am as a Christian is in these eight verses. It defines who Christ is to us, who we are to Christ, and how we are to live as His children. I spend several minutes every day reading just these verses, and since I have to pass by the sitting room to get to the laundry room, I always take the time to pause and look at what I have chosen as my inspiration for not only the room, but for my life.

I would like to be able to say that I have always used these verses as my guide in life but that just isn't so. Like fine wine, I had to age a bit to be able to understand the simplicity of God's word and how to apply it to my life. I wasn't raised in a godly home but thankfully, I had a godly grandmother whose influence from those summer visits stayed with me.

Life can be complicated and as such, I believe we make God and His word just as complicated. I know I did. However, after years of making a mess of my life, I finally decided there had to be a way to

get through my years on earth that didn't
hurt quite so much. I came back to the One
I knew had been there all my life even
through the messes I had made, the trouble I had borrowed, the people I chose to
associate with. God had never left nor for-
saken me (Joshua 1:5), it was I who had
left God. And although He had always been
there, He did leave me to my own defenses
until I finally gave up in the knowledge
that my defenses were pretty flimsy at
best.

John 3:16 says, *"For God so loved
the world that He gave His only begotten
Son, that whoever believes in Him should
not perish but have everlasting life."*

How quickly we tend to forget that
kind of all-encompassing love! How quickly
we pull away and try to do everything on
our own, in our own way. We were never
intended to live apart from God. We were
never intended to be thrown under the bus
of life. Quite the contrary, we were intended to live life fully. To live life loved
beyond measure, (John 10:10). To live life
safely in the arms of God.

We were created in the image of
God in both body (Genesis 1:27) and in

spirit (Ephesians 4:24). We have a God-shaped hole inside of us, yet we spend our lives trying to fill that hole with everything but God! We use sex, drugs, alcohol, rock stars, movie stars, music, sports, fast cars, wealth, food, everything under Heaven except that which we were created for – God.

None of the things of this world can fill that hole God created within us that yearns for Him. Romans 12:2 tells us to not be *"conformed to this world,"* yet, from the time we can crawl, we are fascinated by the things of the world. Not all are bad of course, it's human to want things but it's how we use them, and what we use them for, that defines its worth.

Having money isn't bad. We all need money to live but when money becomes all we think we need, and it becomes all we seek to have, our intentions have gone haywire and money has become our god.

Listening to music isn't bad. Music is pleasurable, relaxing, motivating and part of our being that God put inside of us. But when we begin identifying with lyrics that do not magnify the Lord, or draw our attention away from the important things in our lives, then we've made music our god.

Food is a good thing. We need to eat to stay healthy but when we allow food to become our focus, our bodies begin to rebel. We gain weight, arteries harden, and diabetes can develop, along with heart problems, high cholesterol, and a myriad of other maladies. Food has become our god.

The list goes on. Anything that takes our focus off of God is not good for us. Our spirit weakens, our lives get out of control, and we lose our sense of direction. God is our magnetic north and His Word is our compass. Anytime we allow ourselves to wander off of His course, the life path He has planned for each of us, our lives become something other than what God wants for us. In order to stay on course, we need to be firmly grounded in God's Word. That is the root of our existence. Without a good root system, nothing grows strong.

Anyone who has ever tried to grow plants, flowers, or a vegetable garden, knows that there is a process to getting

13

what you want out of what you plant.
When you grow plants, you expect green
healthy stalks and leaves. With flowers,
you expect tulips from tulip bulbs, roses
from rosebushes, and from a vegetable
garden, you expect each type of vegetable
to produce its own fruit.

But you don't just toss bulbs or
seeds outside on the ground and wait for
them to grow. You till up the ground, you
might have to bring in good soil if you live
in an area like I do. The ground is mostly
rock, and what soil we have is red clay, so
we had to build up garden beds and bring
in soil to fill them. The soil has to have water and fertilizer to be healthy enough for
the plants to develop a good root system.
But they also have to have plenty of sunshine, which is why we plant in springtime
and let the vegetables and flowers grow
through the hot part of summer, and then
harvest in early fall.

Another part of being a gardener is
knowing when to prune. When I go out to
water my garden, I check the plants to
make sure there are no bugs eating them,
no aphids present, and I have to sometimes
prune back some of the leaves and

branches so all the fruit can get plenty of sunshine. Our spirits are like that too. If we don't get plenty of God, His Word, and fellowship with other Christians, we become like the fruit on the bottom of the plants. They grow but they never get quite as ripe or sweet as the other fruit because they don't get the same amount of sun until we prune off some of the leaves.

Malachi 4:2 *"But for you who fear My name, the sun of righteousness will rise with healing in its wings; and you will go forth and skip about like calves from the stall."*

Have you ever seen calves in the fields? They run and leap about like they are so happy just to be there. And when the Lord shines on us, we should leap about with that same kind of joyous abandon! The Lord is our sun. He shines on us with goodness and mercy.

~ * ~

Marie McGaha

Think about it!

Pruning can be painful but it is absolutely necessary in both gardening and in life. If something is not good for us, we have to stop doing it. If we want to be healthy, we have to make changes. The same is true of our Christian walk.

Pray!

Lord, I ask you to show me the things in my life that are not pleasing to you. Show me the areas where I need to make changes so that my life grows the way you want me to. I know your plan for my life is better than anything I can think of and ask that you will lead me in Jesus' Holy Name. Amen.

Decide!

What can you prune from your life to grow in God?

~ Two ~
The Root

As you therefore have received Christ Jesus the Lord, so walk in Him, rooted and built up in Him and established in the faith, as you have been taught, abounding with thanksgiving. Beware lest anyone cheat you through philosophy and empty deceit, according to the tradition of men, according to the basic principles of the world, and not according to Christ.
Colossians 2:6-8

~ * ~

What does it mean to be "rooted" in something? How does one become "rooted"? We know when we plant a seed or bulb, cover it with dirt, water it, and allow the sun to shine on it causes a reaction that sends little tendrils out from the seed. Those tendrils are looking for three things: 1) something firm to hold on to 2) food and 3) water.
But there is something interesting that happens to seeds after they are planted but before those tendrils go out seeking what it needs - the seed dies and rots. It is only after this "death" that the seed begins the process of becoming something else. Like a caterpillar that goes into its chrysalis in order to become a butterfly, you put one thing in the ground and you get something brand new out of it.

So how does a human being become rooted in Christ? How do we go through a "death" process to become something brand new in Him? After all, the Bible does tell us to "...*put on the new man which was created according to God, in true righteousness and holiness*" (Ephesians 4:24), and "...*since you have put off the old man* with his deeds, and have put on the new man who is renewed in knowledge according to the image of Him who created (us)," (Colossians 3:9-10).

John 12:24 – "*Truly, truly, I say to you, unless a grain of wheat falls into the earth and dies, it remains alone, but if it dies, it bears much fruit.*" We have to be like that grain of wheat and die in order to bear fruit. We have to take off our old man and put on our new man.

Galatians 2:20 – "*I have been crucified with Christ. It is no longer I who live, but Christ who lives in me.*"

So we have to die and crucify ourselves in order to live a life pleasing to God – sounds kind of weird, doesn't it? Of course, we are not expected to actually physically die, or to climb up on a cross and let someone nail us to it. The Bible uses these allegorically to emphasize the seriousness of committing one's life to Christ. But if it's not literal, how do we die and crucify ourselves metaphorically? What does it mean to live for Christ? Where do we begin?

The very first step, which I hope you have already taken, is to accept Christ as your Lord and Savior. This step is very easy once you have decided that a life on your own just doesn't work without God. To accept Jesus you pray. Never prayed? That's pretty easy too. Praying is simply talking to God. There's no wrong way to do that. Tell God how you feel. (He already knows.) Tell God you want to change and want a new life with Him. Tell Him you know you've sinned and ask Him to forgive you. Ask Him to live in your heart and to guide you through His Holy Spirit. Then thank Him for doing so.

"If you confess with your mouth the Lord Jesus and believe in your heart that God has raised Him from the dead, you will be saved," (Romans 10:9).

Yes, it really is that simple but that's not all.

Acts 2:38 – *"Then Peter said to them, 'Repent, and let every one of you be baptized in the name of Jesus Christ for the remission of sins, and you shall receive the gift of the Holy Spirit."*

First, God knows all of your sins. He's GOD... He knows everything and there is nothing that you have done that's been hidden from Him. Not even those things you hope no one ever finds out about. God already knows what you've done. He doesn't need an itemized list, He simply wants you to confess that you have sinned and understand your need for forgiveness.

Romans 3:23 - *"For all have sinned and fall short of the glory of God."* That's each and every one of us. We live in a fallen world and are born into sin, but it took just one miracle when Jesus Christ died on the Cross and was raised again on the third day for all of that to be covered in His blood. Jesus died on the Cross for your sins, and for my sins. If you or I were the only person on the face of the earth, we still would have needed Jesus to cover our sins and He would have died just for us. It wasn't a spear in His side that killed Him, it was Jesus' immense and everlasting love for humankind that did.

It was you. It was me. He died because He loved us.

So if you haven't taken that step, please do so now.

Then find a Bible-believing church. A Pentecostal Church is always a good choice. Then talk to the pastor and explain you are a new convert and want to be baptized in water. Even if you were baptized as an infant, you have to be baptized in water again. Baptism alone does not make you sin-free. An infant has not sinned yet, and cannot confess Jesus as Lord, and cannot ask for forgiveness, so they do not need baptism. In fact, baptism without the remission of sins is just a bath!

Water baptism is our identification with Christ's burial and resurrection. We go under the water, our "old man" is buried, we come up out of the water and our "new man" is resurrected. Then pray for the infilling of the Holy Spirit with evidence of speaking in other tongues. (Acts 2:4)

~ * ~

Now that you've accepted Christ as your Savior, you are a new creation. *"Therefore, if anyone is in Christ, he is a new creation; old things have passed away; behold, all things have become new,"* (2 Corinthians 5:17).

This is the essence of "putting off the old man and putting on the new." It means you stop doing the things you used to do and start living a life that is righteous and pleasing to God. To begin with, do what is right. We all know right from wrong, so do right. Get a study Bible and begin by reading the Book of John in the New Testament. It's the fourth book, Matthew, Mark, Luke, John. The Book of John is different than the first three gospels and introduces Jesus Christ in a different way than the other three do. You will get a deeper meaning of who Christ is by reading the Book of John

So what is righteousness? Can a mere human be righteous? And what about that being Holy stuff? *"Because it is written, 'Be Holy for I am Holy,'"* (1 Peter 1:16).

After a lifetime lived in this world, in the sin of this world, being righteous and holy seem like an awful lot to ask. I know it did to me, but that is why we have Christ as our Savior and His Holy Spirit as our guide. We don't have to be righteous on our own because we simply can't be righteous on our own. If we could, God would not have had to send Jesus to live among us and die on the Cross. The entire Old Testament is the history of mankind trying

23

to live in their own righteousness and fail-
ing time after time. Jesus Christ was the
only answer for our fallen state.

Righteous is defined as "1) *of a person or conduct, morally right or justifia-
ble, virtuous, upright, upstanding* 2) *Free
from sin or guilt.*"

That sure didn't describe me before
I accepted Christ as my Savior. I couldn't
have been further from being righteous if I
had tried. But our righteousness is not defined this way; our righteousness comes
from one Source, Jesus. He is our righteousness because He is the only One who
was ever free from sin or guilt. When He
was on the Cross, He took all of our sins
and guilt upon Himself and died for us. His
blood at Calvary covers our sins with love,
and makes us righteous because His shadow
is constantly over us. We walk in His righteousness. We are righteous because we
have accepted Him as Lord and Savior over
our lives, and have given our lives over to
Him.

The root of our salvation is in the
Cross of Christ. The shed blood of Jesus is
our shield and covering against everything
we've ever done. The devil prowls like a

lion, seeking whom he may destroy, (1 Peter 5:8). But he can't even see us through
Christ's blood. He can try to tempt us, to
make life miserable but all we have to say
is, "Look at the Cross, devil. That's the
blood of Jesus covering me!" Even the
devil has to obey God's word, and he prob-
ably knows it better than any person on
earth. He knows how the Bible ends too,
and he loses. Love wins! Christ wins! Those
covered in the love and blood of Christ
win!

The Bible says the word of God is
our sword, (Ephesians 6:17). Read it. Learn
it. Memorize it. Use it. Let God write His
word on the tablet of your heart (Deuter-
onomy 11:18) by memorizing scripture and
taking the time to study His word. And you
will be rooted in God.

~ * ~

Think about it!

Praying is our lifeline to God. Without prayer, we have no communication with the Lord. Prayer is mentioned over three hundred times in the Bible, and Christ prayed many times in the New Testament. If Jesus felt the need to pray, how much more important is prayer in our life?

Pray!jer

Lord, I don't always pray as much as I should. I sometimes think that I can handle everything on my own, or I think my problems just aren't that important to you. Forgive me for not depending on you, for not praying in every circumstance, and help me to see that you are interested in everything I do. Teach me to pray and depend on you. In Jesus' Holy Name, Amen.

Decide!

What can you do to improve your prayer life?

~ Three ~
Sowing Your Own Seed

As you have therefore received Christ Je-
sus
The Lord, so walk in Him, rooted and built
up in Him and established in the faith as
you have been taught
Abounding in it with thanksgiving.
Colossians 2:6-7

~ * ~

The world we live in is in total op-
position to a life in Christ Jesus. In the
world, we are taught to be independent,
don't rely on anyone, get up and do it
yourself, pull yourself up by your boot-
straps, but a life in Christ is total dependence upon Him. John 15:1-8 is all about
dependence rather than independence, yet
being dependent upon Jesus is the most
freedom a person will ever have. Sounds
like a contradiction but it isn't. The pas-
sage in John tells us that Christ is the vine
and we are the branches, and apart from
Him, we can do nothing. Jesus is our root
system, He is what holds us firmly in place,
grounded when everything in the world
seems to be spinning out of control. In
Him, we live and move and have our being
(Acts 17:29).

Have you noticed what happens to a
branch that gets ripped away from the
vine? It dies. There is no nourishment from
the roots, so instead of that branch contin-
uing to grow and produce fruit, it withers
and dies. The branch is useless away from
vine. So it is with us. Nothing we do in life,
no matter what kind of success we might

have, no matter how much money we make, or how famous we become, none of it is worth anything if we are not connected to the Vine that is Jesus Christ.

The rich and famous have problems, perhaps more problems than the rest of us. They have addiction problems, their children are out of control, they are unhappy and seem to have no direction. That's because all of the riches and fame in the world cannot produce satisfaction in the soul. True satisfaction can only come from one place, and that's from the Lord. We have to fill that God-shaped hole with God. Nothing else fits. Nothing else satisfies because our spirits are created to worship only One. When we worship at the feet of the gods of this world, we cannot find the peace we desire, or the satisfaction our souls search desperately for.

"For what profit is it to a man if he gains the whole world and loses his own soul?" (Matthew 16:26).

How many Hollywood "stars" have we seen take their own lives, overdose on drugs, be victims of murder, or have their lives so out of control they become jokes on late night talk shows? Money, fame, and

success does not equal happiness and contentment. Very few "stars" stand up for
what is right and good and pure. Very few
will speak about God, and the few Christian "stars" in Hollywood are ostracized by
the rest.

We see famous politicians, business-
men and women, people who are known
for nothing but being rich who face the
very same problems in their lives as the
rest of us. Money is not a cure for what is
wrong in our lives. Fame is not the cure ei-
ther. If it was, those rich and famous people would not be in such pain and turmoil.
The only cure for our souls, for the world
as it is today, is a right relationship with
God Almighty through His Son Jesus Christ.

*"From whence does my help come?
My help comes from the Lord, who made
Heaven and earth."* (Psalm 121:1)

Our only real, lasting help comes
from Jesus Christ. He is the only One who
can save us from ourselves, the world, and
what is to come after our physical deaths.
Afraid to die? If you don't know Jesus as
your Savior, you better be! What comes after this life is eternity. Forever and ever
and ever... A time that we cannot even

truly understand. Eternity is infinite, without end, no time, no calendar, no concept
of life as we now know it. Yet we will live
eternally. After we die here, and we are
all going to die, our souls leave our bodies
and go to eternity. Where that eternity is
spent is totally up to us.

    *"If you confess with your mouth...
you will be saved,"* (Roman 10:9). If you
have accepted Christ as your Savior and
made Him Lord of your life, you are saved.
You will spend eternity in Heaven experi-
encing the Lord in a way we cannot even
comprehend in this life. It will be joyous,
wonderful, and beyond words. We will be
with our friends and family who went before us, as long as they also knew Jesus as
their Savior. If we had young children or in-
fants who passed away, they will be there
waiting to welcome us. I have a son, three
daughters, a step-daughter, and three
grandsons who are in Heaven awaiting my
arrival. My grandmother is there too. What
a family reunion that is going to be! The
Bible says we will *"know as we are
known,"* (1 Corinthians 13:12). That means
we will know one another just as we know
them now on earth in this life. But more

Marie McGaha

important-ly, we will see Christ face-to-face and we will know Him as He is, (1 John 3:2).

However, if we have not known Christ as our Savior while we have the chance here on earth in this life, we will not live out eternity in Heaven with Him. We will spend eternity in a place that is truly beyond any horrors we can imagine. A place of torment, a place described as a *"lake that burns with fire and brimstone,"* (Revelation 21:8). And Revelation 20:15 tells us, *"Anyone not found written in the Book of Life was cast into the lake of fire."* And that also lasts for eternity. There is no backing out once you have passed from this life to the afterlife. You will stand before God, both the righteous and unrighteous, and give an account for your life on earth (2 Corinthians 5:10). God is only going to allow people into Heaven who are covered in the blood of Jesus, who confessed Him as their Lord and Savior while alive on earth. You cannot do it after death. Make sure your name is written in the Book of Life.

So what is this Book of Life and how do you get your name in it? That is the easy

32

part! Heaven keeps a record of each and every one of us, whether for life or death. Nothing we say or do gets by God, (Matthew 12:36). However, when we accept Jesus Christ as our Lord and Savior, all of Heaven rejoices and the Angel of the Lord writes our names in the Lambs Book of Life, (Revelation 21:27). The twenty-first chapter of Revelation is a look at Heaven and it's beautiful, more beautiful than what John was able to describe, I'm sure. I cannot imagine anyone not wanting to be in Heaven. There is nothing on this earth that is worth forfeiting one's soul, nothing worth having outside of a relationship with Jesus Christ because once you have that relationship, you have everything!

There is nothing that can happen to you that is out of Jesus' control. Even the bad things that happen in life, things we don't understand, things that cause us grief and pain, none of them are outside of the help and love of Jesus. We live in a fallen world that, short of every human on earth bowing before Heaven and confessing Christ is Lord, is going to cause us distress at some point in life. We will still lose loved ones, we will still lose jobs, not have enough money, or watch our children stray, among all of the other millions of things we face in everyday life.

The difference between Christians and non-Christians is how we deal with life. A Christian has the assurance that 1) God is in control 2) We are His 3) He makes ALL things work together for our good (Romans 8:28). So if ALL things work together, that includes the bad situations. There is nothing God cannot do, is not willing to do, or won't do for us who love Him and have been sanctified through the blood of His precious Son, Jesus.

~ * ~

Marie McGaha

Think about it!

The world is not out to help you or make your life better. The world is out to get you! There is nothing more difficult than trying to get through life on your own, it's like trying to paddle upstream. It's frustrating, tiring, and it will drag you down. Living a life in Christ Jesus does not keep us from having bad days but it will keep the world from dragging us down. The world is against us, but Christ is for us!

Pray!

Lord, I have tried living this life on my own and I have failed time after time. I know the world offers nothing but heartache and distraction from what you want for me. I pray you will guide me to know your will in my life, that I might serve you and others. I pray that no matter what I see in life, I will remember that it is your will and not mine, and like you, I will be about my father's business. I pray in Jesus' Holy Name. Amen.

Decide!

What is going on in your life that isn't of God? Are you trying to walk with one foot in the world and the other in church? Make the decision for Christ today in all areas of your life!

~ *Four* ~
The Master of the Vineyard

*Then He spoke many things to them in par-
ables, saying: "Behold, a sower went out
to sow, and as he sowed, some seed fell by
the wayside and birds came and devoured
them. Some fell on stony places, where
they did not have much earth, and they
immediately sprang up because they had
no depth of earth. But when the sun was
up they were scorched, and because they
had no root they withered away. And some
fell among thorns, and the thorns sprang
up and choked them. But others fell on
good ground and yielded a good crop: some
a hundredfold, some sixty, some thirty."*
Matthew 13:3-8

~ * ~

Jesus taught in parables to help us remember His words and to help us have a greater understanding of His teachings. In the above parable we see four scenarios of seed being planted. The first three resulted in nothing but the last was very successful. Later in the same chapter, verses 18-23, Jesus goes on to explain. We find that the "seed" is the Word of God, the ground is our hearts, and the result of planting the seed depends solely on our willingness and readiness to hear and believe. The first is described as someone who received the Word of God "by the wayside" and what was sown in his heart was taken away by the devil. The second, sown on "stony ground" is the person who receives the Word of God with joy but because he "has no root," as soon as the trials of life come along, he abandons the truths of God and tries to take care of the situation on his own. The third seed is someone who hears the Word of God but "the cares and the deceitfulness of this world" are more important to him and he allows them to choke the truth of Jesus out of his life.

Finally, the last one is a person who is ready to hear, accept, believe, and live the Word of God. This person becomes fruitful, producing a "crop" up to a hundredfold what he was given. This is the person I hope that I am. This is the person that I hope we can all be. But what does it mean to produce a crop and be fruitful? How do we take an intangible and turn it into something tangible? When you under-stand that your life is unmanageable on your own and that the only answer is Je-sus, your heart becomes that good and fer-tile ground where good seed will grow and produce fruit.

I never considered myself to have any talent. My father, grandfather, uncles all had talent. My father plays guitar and sings. My grandfather could play any stringed instrument you placed in his hands. My dad's cousin, David, who spoke with a stutter, could play guitar and when he sang, his voice never faltered. David's brother, Mel, was an artist. He could paint anything you asked him to. I can't draw a straight line without a ruler and I can't carry a tune to save my life. Compared to these family members, I had no talent. It bothered me all of my life. The funny thing was, I have always been a writer.

As a child, I wrote simple stories to entertain myself, and as a teen I wrote the requisite morose poetry. I was thirteen when I wrote my first book. It was set in the Wild West about a school teacher who came from Boston and fell in love with the local sheriff. As a young mom I wrote stories for my children but I never considered that a "talent." To me, talent meant playing an instrument, painting the Sistine Chapel, composing an overture, or writing the great American novel like John Steinbeck. It took me an entire lifetime to understand that talent is in all of us.

It takes talent to raise a family and run a household. It takes talent to be a mechanic, a carpenter, a farmer, a rancher, a teacher, a doctor, and anything else that is in our hearts to do. Talent isn't defined by the world's recognition of what we do but rather, by our recognition of what God wants us to do *for* Him.

A person who desires to become a missionary in a third-world country has a specific talent. The Sunday school teacher has just as much talent as the person who plays the piano during worship. The youth leader has just as much talent as the pastor who leads the church body.

1 Corinthians 12:12-31 talks about the church body being one, yet made up of many members. It goes on to say the body couldn't function if all the members were a foot, or a hand, or an eye. It takes all the members working together for the body to function properly, with one Head, Jesus Christ. Whatever your talent is, it is needed in the body of Christ.

If we all painted, the world might be pretty but we would certainly be bored with it. If we all played an instrument, the world would sound better but I doubt we'd be entertained for any length of time. We need each other, and each other's specific talents in order to be a complete body. We need preachers to preach the Word of God to us. We need those who play instruments and sing to lead us in worship. We need those among us who have the desire to heal because we need doctors and nurses. We need moms who keep the homes, we need dads who go to work every day to keep the bills paid. It is in these every day talents that we produce our own type of fruit.

Whatever we do in the Lord is going to produce a wonderful harvest. We are told in Colossians 3:17 – *"And whatever you do in word or deed, do all in the name of the Lord Jesus, giving thanks to God the Father through Him."* And in verses 23 & 24 – *"And whatever you do, do it heartily, as to the Lord and not to men, knowing that from the Lord you will receive the reward of the inheritance; for you serve the Lord Christ."* Our God-given talents are going to produce not just fruit, but it will gain us the inheritance of life everlasting in Heaven.

When we accept Christ as our Savior, we are in essence, giving our lives over to Him, knowing that we can trust Him fully to always do what is best for us. So it becomes our duty, out of love for Him, to give our best back to Him in all that we do.

No matter what job we have, whether a waitress, a janitor, a doctor or president of a company, we must bring our A-game every single day. It is our duty to Christ and because of what He did for us that we be shining examples of who He is, *not* who we are. We must show godliness in everything we say and do. Our speech must be soft and loving. Our actions must show prudence and gentleness. Our work must be done with gladness of heart, knowing that no job is beneath us or above us. If we do all as if "unto the Lord" as our verses above tell us to, people around us will see Christ in us and that will produce the fruit of witnessing. And that is our main job – to show Christ to the world around us.

We are told to be "Christ-like," which sounds rather daunting since He was perfect and we are not. But we are not being Christ-like in and of ourselves, we are simply allowing Christ to shine through us in word and actions. In a hurting world, seeing someone who is at peace with themselves, at peace with the world, who is not worried about anything, and who does not fear the future, is someone that people are attracted to. They will want to know why you're different and that will give you the opportunity to tell them – I am redeemed by the Lord of lords, rescued by the King of kings, and I have a glorious and wonderful future!

Our fruit, that which we produce in our lives in day-to-day living is brought about by living like Christ, by having Christ live through us. When people we know see that we have changed, that ungodly speech is gone from our mouths, that ungodly living is gone from our lives, that our marriages are working out when divorce was knocking on the door, that our children are behaving when they weren't before, when we receive promotions and raises at a job we used to complain about, when we radiate happiness, joy, and peace no matter what situation arises in our lives, that is appealing to others. In a hurting world, we know that we may have to live in this world, but we are not part of it (John 17:16).

~ * ~

Marie McGaha

Think about it!

Just because we think we have
nothing to offer, no particular talent or
ability, doesn't mean it's true. Each of us
has a place in the Kingdom of God, and
each of us has something to offer. We can
serve God in many ways, not just by
preaching, teaching, singing, or playing an
instrument. There is a place that only you
can serve and no one else can fill that
place the way you can!

Pray!

Lord, I don't believe I have much
talent, and when I look around the world, I
see talent in everyone but myself. I ask
that You would show me where my talent
lies, and how You want me to serve You.
Guide me by Your Holy Spirit and help me
to see myself the way that You do. In Jesus' Holy Name. Amen.

Marie McGaha

Decide!

Jesus came as a servant, and if nothing else, we can serve others. Visiting nursing homes, volunteering at a soup kitchen, cleaning house for sick church member... That is real talent! Don't let the devil rob you of the blessings that comes from having a servant's heart!

~ Five ~
The Root and Offspring

"I, Jesus, have sent my angel to testify
these things in the churches. I am the Root
and the Offspring of David, the Bright and
Morning Star."
Revelation 22:16

~ * ~

Jesus is our everything. Our morning, our day, our night, our moon, our stars
and the sun. He is the weeks, months and
years. He is everything, in everything,
above everything. He is our all and in all
(Colossians 3:11). Even so, many people
are very willing to allow Jesus to be their
Savior, to accept the offer of salvation and
guarantee their place in Heaven but few
are willing to allow Him to actually be
their "all". What exactly does it mean to
allow Christ complete, unfettered access
to our lives? That requires a level of trust
that I could not give to anyone when I was
living life on my own.

However, when I decided to follow
Jesus, I also decided I was going in the
deep end. I wasn't going to be happy with
simply saying "I'm saved" but not have
everything God has to offer. I wasn't going
to be someone who lived my life all week
long and filled a seat in church on Sunday,
and at Easter and Christmas. I wanted everything. But that's who I am. When I lived
in the world, I dove in head first. When I
drank, I drank to excess. When I used
drugs, I became an addict. When I opened

my mouth, the worst things came out of it. When I went into a bar, sailors ran out – okay, that's an exaggeration but I really was a great sinner. I sinned in every way imaginable and I broke God's heart, so when I came to my senses (read about King Nebuchadnezzar in Daniel Chapter 4, and pay attention to verse 34), and accepted Christ as my Savior, I could not disrespect the Lord by not pursuing Heaven with even more enthusiasm as I did when pursing hell.

And that is what we are all doing outside of a relationship with Jesus Christ. We are pursuing hell. We are pursuing damnation. We are pursuing eternity separated from our Maker because of stubbornness, selfishness, and the refusal to acknowledge that left to our own devices, we fail miserably. It doesn't matter what your position in life is, whether a beggar on the street or sitting in a palace, if you are not pursuing God with all that you are, you are pursuing hell.

That includes "good" people. I've heard so many people say that their loved one went to Heaven because they were so good. I'm sorry but being "good" does not

get you into Heaven any more than being
"bad" sends you to hell. That might come
as a shock to many but our goodness
doesn't even rate on the God scale. Isaiah
64:6 - *"But we are like an unclean thing,
and all our righteousnesses are like filthy
rags..."* This is strong talk from Isaiah because that term "filthy rags" refers to the
rags women used while having their peri-
ods. What a comparison!

Daniel 5:27 – *"Tekel: You have been
weighed and found wanting."* When I stand
before the Lord of the universe, I do not
want to hear those words. I want to hear,
*"Well done thou good and faithful serv-
ant..."* – Matthew 25:21, 23.

In the sermon Holy Ambition, the
author, Chip Ingram, points out that while
most Christians will say they want to hear
these words from Christ, most are unwill-
ing to actually do what is necessary to en-
sure hearing those words.

What does it take to be a good and
faithful servant of the Lord Jesus Christ?

Luke 9:23-24 - *Then He said to
them, "If anyone desires to come after
Me, let him deny himself, and take up his*

cross daily and follow me. For whoever desires to save his life will lose it, but whoever loses his life for My sake will save it."

Denying our natural self is what it takes. We have to live with an attitude of servitude, which is how Jesus lived on earth. He wasn't here to promote Himself, but to promote the Kingdom of Heaven and to serve the people He met on a daily basis. He loved everyone. He showed kindness, caring, and had the attitude of a servant. He didn't put Himself above anyone and He never told anyone they were too much of a sinner to follow Him.

The woman found guilty of adultery was about to be stoned to death but Jesus did not condemn her. The people who came to Him asking for healing, He gave to them. He raised Lazarus from the dead – four days in the grave. He fed the hungry, He cast out demons, and He answered the legalist Pharisees who tried to trick Him. But the one thing He didn't do was condemn anyone because of the way they dressed, the job they had, or the sins they committed. If we truly desire to follow Jesus, we have to treat everyone the way Jesus did. We have to love them and help them in whatever way we are able. If we can feed the hungry, then that's what we do. If we can offer comfort to someone who is hurting, then we offer comfort. If we can offer medical care, then we offer medical care. If we can do nothing else, we can love others and show them compassion no matter who they are. And we can most certainly pray for everyone.

Verse 26 says, *"For whoever is ashamed of Me and My words, of him, the Son of Man will be ashamed..."*

Lord forgive me if I ever acted like I was ashamed of you! Of all the things I've done in my life that I can be ashamed of, Jesus is not one of them. I think those of us who have been on the lowest side of low understand our need for salvation and how deeply we need the love of Christ. Our need is no greater than the need for salvation that anyone else has but I think we have a greater understanding of that need simply because we can identify with people like Paul, who persecuted the followers of Christ, and the adulterous woman who knew Jesus had saved her from certain death.

I love the story I heard about Jeffrey Dahmer, the serial killer who was killed in prison by another inmate. I pray the story is true and I believe it is because it came from his mother following his death.

Jeffrey Dahmer's mother was a Christian and raised her son in the Assembly of God Church. She said he was saved, had accepted Christ as his Savior at an early age but somewhere along the way, Jeff got lost. Just like we all do. Jeff's life went way off course and he wound up being a notorious serial killer, a villain most people wanted to shoot on sight. Jeff was killed when another inmate stabbed him with a broken mop handle. The great part of this story is that Jeff's mom went to visit him often and took her Bible with her. She prayed with him and read Scripture with him. She said that a few weeks before he was killed, Jeffrey Dahmer had accepted the Lord as his Savior. Jeffrey Dahmer was murdered for who he was, but upon his death, the Lord welcomed him in Heaven with open arms.

Some have told me that is a terrible story. I've heard people say that if Jeffrey

Dahmer was in Heaven, they didn't want to be. And "How could God allow someone like that in Heaven?" I know this, God does not judge us by our sins but by whether or not we accepted His Son, Jesus Christ, as our Lord and Savior. He will forgive anyone no matter what they have done, no matter the vile acts they've committed, if they approach the Throne with a contrite spirit and a heart ready to accept Christ.

God does not weigh sin the same way the world does. In our world, the courts judge crimes according to their merit. Shoplifting gets a slap on the wrist, bank robbery carries some federal time, murder can get life without parole, or even the death penalty. But to God, sin is sin. No sin is greater than any other, hell awaits liars, murderers, sexual deviants, those who have used the Lord's Name in vain, in essence, hell awaits anyone who does not accept Christ as their Savior to turn their life around.

Seems kind of harsh. But when you realize that God is HOLY and cannot look upon sin of any kind, you realize that the nastiness of this world deserves nothing

more than hell. Yet, here we are, imperfect people, in an imperfect world, living
imperfect lives with a God who sent His
own Son so that we would not have to get
what we deserve. That's mercy, that's
grace in action, that's love.

Many years ago, I was told that
mercy is God not giving us what we deserve, grace is deliverance through salvation. I do not deserve Heaven. I do not deserve salvation. Yet, I have both because
of mercy and grace. God gave us mercy
when He sent Christ to earth. Jesus gave us
grace when He died on the Cross.

I don't want to ever go back to the
life I led before. I can't imagine anyone
would. I want to be a servant of the Lord
that is received by Christ with open arms
when I step out of this life and into the
next. I don't want anyone to look at me in
this life and see anyone but Jesus. I don't
want to open my mouth except that the
words of the Lord come out. I want every
action in my life to reflect who I am, who I
am becoming, as a follower of Jesus. I
want people to see HIM when they look at
me. And I do that by reading His word, by
studying, by memorizing, by going to

church, by fellowship with other believers, through praise and worship.

Paul says in Philippians 3:14 – *"I press toward the goal for the prize of the upward call of God in Christ Jesus."*

I can imagine no higher calling in my life than this: to follow after Jesus with all that is within me, to serve Him in whatever way He calls me, to be firmly grounded, rooted in Him and His Word, and to produce the fruit this calling has for me.

~ * ~

Marie McGaha

Think about it!

Have you ever looked at someone and thought there's no way they'll ever get to Heaven? Is it because you know their particular sins? Is it because they look different than what you think a Christian should look like? Is it their dress, hygiene, or lifestyle? When a Holy God looks at us, we all look the same. We are pitiful and weak and undeserving of God's grace and mercy. There isn't a single one of us that is any different than anyone else. We are born into a world of sin and unless God cleans up our inside, we are no more deserving of Heaven than anyone else.

Pray!

Lord, I know I don't deserve Your grace or mercy. I don't deserve Heaven. I know that I deserve to go hell but I thank You for Your salvation, for having pity on me, for calling me Your own. Help me to see others the way You see me, as someone who deserves the love that only You can provide. Help to know the words to say, and give me a heart that seeks to be as kind to others as You have been to me. In Jesus' Holy Name. Amen.

Decide!

People everywhere are hurting. Drugs, alcohol, violence, has taken over our world and sometimes it's difficult to have hope that anything can change. But you are the change you want to see in the world. Who can you show mercy and grace to today?

~ Six ~
The True Vine

"I am the true vine, and My Father
is the vinedresser. Every branch in Me
that does not bear fruit He takes away;
and every branch that bears fruit He
prunes, that it may bear more fruit. You
are already clean because of the word
which I have spoken to you. Abide in Me,
and I in you. As the branch cannot bear
fruit of itself, unless it abides in the vine,
neither can you, unless you abide in Me."
John 15:1-4

~ * ~

When a garden is planted, and the seeds are covered in good earth, the tiny tendrils reach out for nourishment, then the tiny shoot pushes upward, reaching toward the sky, toward the sun. Over time, it gets bigger, stronger, and taller until it flowers and those flowers mature and turn into tomatoes, cucumbers, peppers, watermelon, or whatever type of seed was planted. But none of that would happen if the plant wasn't firmly rooted in the ground. The root system is everything to the plant, and so Jesus must be everything to us. Without being planted firmly in Jesus, we have no hope of reaching forward, reaching upward, and producing fruit.

When I was in Antlers, Oklahoma, Pastor Jerry Vickers from New Life Apostolic Church taught on The Temple from the book of Exodus. It was an excellent study but something Pastor said one night really hit home. He was talking about the Table of Showbread, which led to Jesus being the Bread of Life. Jesus says, *"I am the bread of life. He who comes to Me shall never hunger, and he who believes in Me shall never thirst,"* (John 6:35). He then went on to explain that we must consume the Word of God on a daily basis. That means reading God's Word, studying God's Word, getting it down inside of us where it will stick and be ever-present in our minds and our thinking.

Further down in that same chapter, verse 51 says, *"I am the living bread which came down from Heaven. If anyone eats of this bread, he will live forever; and the bread that I shall give is My flesh, which I shall give for the life of the world."*

Verses 53-54: Then Jesus said to them, *"Most assuredly, I say to you, unless you eat the flesh of the Son of Man and drink His blood, you have no life in you. Whoever eats My flesh and drinks My blood has eternal life, and I will raise him up at the last day."*

So how do we do that? First, once we believe Jesus is the Christ and have faith to believe and accept Him as our Savior, we already have part in eternal life. Second, as Christians, we partake in the Communion ceremony of eating the unleavened bread and drinking grape juice when it is served in church. Third, we devour God's Word.

I think with accepting Christ as our Savior being the most important thing that we do, devouring God's Word is a very close second. There are sixty-six books in the Bible and there is an answer for every problem in our lives within those pages. I have read the Bible several times over and it never gets boring. I learn something new every time I read it. And no matter what is going on in my life, there is always an answer from God in those pages.

When I read a work of fiction, or even non-fiction, I rarely read it twice. There are some books I really liked and read more than once but I get the same thing out of them the second time as I did the first. The story is meant to evoke certain emotions and hopefully, have a tidy ending where all the parts come together for an emotionally satisfying finish. I don't get answers to life's really important questions from my leisure reading. I get entertained for a couple of hours, which is the intent.

However, the Bible is completely different. Everything we need to know about life, how to live it, deal with it, live with other people, how to raise our children, how to stay happily married, and especially, how to have more from life than just getting up and going to bed. The Bible gives us life lessons on everything we can ever imagine encountering in real life, and gives us not just joy in this life but confidence that this is not all there is, and there is more to the heavens than just the sun, moon and stars. God's Word is not the invention of any man but straight from the Heart of Heaven to the ears of mankind. God did not just make us and then leave us to our own devices. He set before us a life plan that works for our good no matter what giants we face.

I live on a small farm usually by myself because my husband is a truck driver and is gone much of the time. It is up to me to care for the animals, do the planting, weeding, and watering, gather the eggs, buck the hay, keep the fences up, and clean house, cook for and clean up after ten dogs, pay the bills, haul the garbage, and everything else that goes along with life. The biggest problem I have is that I was born with a bone and joint disease and spent over a year in a wheel chair

in my early 30's prior to my first two surgeries. I've had three hip surgeries, and
neck surgery, plus my spinal column and
every joint in my body is disintegrating due
to this disease. I also have arthritis
throughout my body but especially in my
hands, feet and back, and I have carpel
tunnel syndrome in both wrists. I am in
pain more often than not and doing farm
chores exacerbates these problems. I also
fall down a lot—partly because of the joint
disease and partly because I am a world-
class klutz.

   I would love to have been born
"normal", without these physical problems
but part of my abilities as an author, wife,
mother, and follower of Christ has come
due to these problems. I have been prayed
over more times than I can possibly count
that the Lord would heal me. I have
prayed, and asked, and knocked and
knocked on Heaven's Door asking the Lord
to heal me. And I received the same answer as Paul, *"And he said to me, 'My
grace is sufficient for you, my strength is
made perfect in weakness, '"* (2 Corinthians
12:9).

Does that mean God doesn't love me because He hasn't healed me? Does it mean I've done something wrong? Of course not. I think God hasn't healed me because I am a bulldozer, and without the affliction of this bone disease, I may never have come to Him. I am strong-willed, determined, self-sufficient, I don't ask for help, I know what I want and I don't stop till I get it, and according to my mother, I'm as bullheaded as a person can get. I've been that way since I was a toddler. My mother says I was born as an adult. I never wanted to be a kid, I wanted to be a grown up, and I never listened to anyone. I did exactly what I wanted, when I wanted, how I wanted. I am a bulldozer.

That is not always a good thing. Especially when I was young and not really as smart as I thought I was. I hurt other people and I hurt myself. I got into situations I couldn't get out of, and I wound up face first in the mud on several occasions. But God makes us who we are, He sets those traits within us, it's learning to use them according to His example that's the hard part, or at least it was for me. I thank God that I survived my own stubborn, hardheaded ways and didn't die in my stupidity and unbelief. I can look back now and see God beside me every crooked step I took. I can see how He used my pain, surgeries and sufferings as a way to make me sit still long enough that He could get me to pay attention to Him. If I had not been born with a disease that put me in a wheelchair, I might have never listened to God at all because I would have never stop-ped running long enough to hear Him.

Now I am in such bad shape that walking is very difficult. I am in pain most all of the time, and I get through each chore, each hour, each day being fully de-pendent on God. I wake up and praise God that I got to sleep, which I don't do much of anymore. I put my feet on the floor and ask God to give me the strength to stand, to walk, to get through the day ahead. And He does. When the chores are finished, I spend the rest of the day devouring God's Word.

I read the Bible. I have Bible apps on my phone for my daily devotionals, prayers, advice, and Christian worship mu-sic. I pray and spend time with God because I know He is my source of life, comfort, strength, wisdom, vision for future books, and the reason I am alive today. My pastor said he wished he had memorized God's Word when he was younger because he can't just pull a verse out of memory anymore, and I understand that. I wish the same thing. I wish I had committed my life and mind to the Lord when I was a youngster because after all the drugs and alcohol in my younger days, I have a hard time memorizing anything.

Devour God's Word. Let it fill your mind, heart and spirit. Let your soul rest in the Word of God, and even if you're like me and can't pull chapter and verse out of your head, you will know the words because God will give them to you when you need them. I can't tell you how many times I've repeated the Words of the Lord in a situation because God gave them to me. I couldn't have told anyone which book of the Bible they came from but I knew the words because I've read them so often, they are a part of me.

Jesus Christ loves us so much, He died so that we might be able to spend eternity in Heaven with Him. When I read

the Bible and pray, and I hear that still,
small voice and God's Spirit is all around
me, and my spirit resonates with His, I can
do nothing but praise Him and thank Him
for what He has done in my life.

~ * ~

Think about it!

True freedom lies in a godly life. It is within these parameters that God's blessings flow. While we all like to have things our own way sometimes, being willful can and does get us into trouble. Even Christians have to keep the "self" in check, freedom in Christ is not freedom to do whatever we want. It's not always easy but it is always worth it.

Pray!

Lord, sometimes my nature gets the best of me. Sometimes I say things I shouldn't, sometimes I get angry, sometimes I have attitude, and I know these are from the flesh. I pray Lord that You would renew my strength and set a right spirit within me. Remind me when I am not acting in a way that is pleasing to You, and cause me to seek a new attitude that glorifies you. In Jesus' Name, Amen.

Decide!

Attitude is everything! What can you do to keep a right attitude?

~ Seven ~
The Fruit of the Spirit

"But the fruit of the Spirit is love, joy, peace, longsuffering (patience), kindness, goodness, faithfulness, gentleness, self-control. Against such there is no law."
Galatians 5:22-23

~ * ~

When we talk about the "fruit of the Spirit" we are talking about character traits that develop within us as a result of following Christ. We are told to be like Christ, to walk as He did and to speak as He did. We are told to *"have the mind of Christ,"* (1 Corinthians 2:16); to offer our *"bodies as a living sacrifice,"* to *"not be conformed to this world,"* (Romans 12:1-2); and to *"conduct yourselves in a manner worthy of the gospel of Christ,"* (Philippians 1:27).

Jesus left some pretty big footprints for us to fill in His Name. But He did not leave us to do it alone. He left us His Holy Spirit as our Comforter and Helper, (John 14:26). But it doesn't happen on its own, we have to set our wills, our minds to accomplishing this task. We have to study God's Word, practice what the Bible says, and *"work out (our) salvation daily,"* (Philippians 2:12). As we go through this world following Christ, we will develop a Christ-like character and produce the fruit of the Spirit.

The first trait listed is love. This is not the type of love most of us are familiar with. We know the love we feel for our parents, our spouse, our children, or our pets, but this is not the love God has for us, and not the love God expects *from* us. This type of love is called *Agape* love. *Agape* is a Greek word that means "the highest form of love, charity; the love God has for man, and man for God. *Agape* embraces a universal, unconditional love that transcends, that serves regardless of circumstances."

The second trait is joy. This does not mean being happy, although, once we are saved, we have a lot to be happy about but the Bible is talking about something much deeper than happiness. According to *Theopedia*, "Joy is a state of mind and an orientation of the heart. A settled state of contentment, confidence and hope." Jesus says in John 15:11, *"These things I have spoken to you that My joy may remain in you, and that your joy may be full."* Joy is not an emotion, it is a state of being.

Next is peace. Most of us relate the word peace as being the opposite of war. However, the peace we have in Jesus Christ is akin to joy. It is what happened when Christ died on the Cross for all of humankind. Christ's death brought peace between God and man. It brought unity and purity between a Holy God and fallen man. Without the peace of Christ, we could never have been reconciled with God. It is not the absence of turmoil in the world but rather, the ability for those who accept Christ to live in an imperfect world with perfect peace.

Longsuffering, or patience, from God's perspective is indeed different than how the world defines patience. Godly patience is a virtue that allows Christians to endure suffering, wrongs, and evil without complaining. The way God has been patient in waiting for mankind to accept Christ as their Savior because *it is not God's desire that any should perish*," (2 Peter 3:9).

Kindness would seem to be self-explanatory, however, God has a different standard for kindness. The Greek word here is *chrestos*. Part of the meaning is defined as "useful", something that requires action, just like love. It isn't what you say, it's what you *do*.

Goodness is next in our verse. What is goodness? Is it just being good, as in not being bad? Or is there a deeper meaning? While we use the word "good" to describe a variety of things, such as "good job", have a "good day", to determine if food tastes good, or if it has spoiled, "is the milk still good", or your child got "good grades". As you can see, "good" is another word we throw around depending on our need for it. However, God determines "goodness" as virtue. Virtue is defined as "righteousness, morality, integrity, and dignity." Quite a difference!

Next is the fruit of faithfulness. We understand faithfulness as someone who doesn't cheat on their spouse, someone who goes to church every week, someone who is faithful to their exercise routine, their job, or anything that we do persistently. God is faithful in everything He says and does. He does not fail us and does not lie. We too must be faithful to God in keeping our vows to Him, but also to the people in our lives. We must always do what we say we will and keep our promises.

Baker's Evangelical Dictionary defines our next trait, gentleness, as "sensitivity of disposition and kindness of behavior, founded on strength and prompted by love." In action, gentleness is how we treat one another.

Self-control. In the world today, this seems to be lacking everywhere. Self-control, according to God, is keeping your tongue under control, keeping our desires under control, and not giving in to the worldly urges that we may experience.

The fruit of the Spirit is what occurs in us when we walk with Jesus and practice being Christ-like.

~ * ~

Think about it!

Self-control! We all know about the terrible twos and the dreaded teen years when self-control is out of control. It's expected in two year old, tolerated in hormonal teens but we expect them to outgrow the tantrums. When an adult has a tantrum, it's not very pretty. In fact, it's ridiculous! Yet, we see more and more of this behavior on social media from celebrities and every day, normal people. It seems like acting out is the newest fad. But what it really shows is people who are selfish and have no concern for others and no self-respect. It shows just how much this world opposes everything the Bible teaches.

Pray!

Lord, help me to learn more about You and Your ways, to desire those things that please you and show the world a different way to live. Grow the fruit of Your Spirit within me so that others may see You an desire to also know You. Help me to be the light this world needs in order to help

others. Let everything in my life be a bless-
ing and not a hindrance and if there is anything in my life that is not pleasing to You,
reveal it to me. In Jesus' Name. Amen.

Decide!

What spiritual fruit are you grow-
ing?

Marie McGaha

~ Eight ~
Love

"Beloved, let us love one another for love
is of God, and everyone who loves is born
of God and knows God. He who does not
love does not know God, for God is love. In
this the love of God was manifested toward us that God has sent His only begotten Son into the world that we might live
through Him. In this is love, not that we
loved God, but that He loved us and sent
His Son to be the propitiation for our sins.
Beloved, if God so loved us, we also ought
to love one another."
1 John 4:7-11

~ * ~

Jesus Christ is pure love given by God to redeem a corrupt and perverse world. When we accept Him as our Savior, we are accepting the love of God.

God loves us regardless of our circumstances, sins, and transgressions, no matter what. God loves us so much that He sent His only begotten Son to suffer and die for us, so we have the opportunity to be forgiven of our sins and have eternity in Heaven. Christ voluntarily came to earth, gave up glory, took on a finite human body, subjected Himself to ridicule, torture and a horrible death just so that we can have the opportunity to follow Him, and live for Him on earth, and with Him in eternity.

"But God demonstrates His own love toward us, in that while we were still sinners, Christ died for us. Much more then, having now been justified by His blood, we shall be saved from wrath through Him," (Romans 5:8-9).

That is true love. Pure love. Love that sees past our human frailty and to the righteousness of Christ without wanting anything in return except to be loved back.

How great is God! And to have that kind of
love, that redemptive love of Christ that
forgives us of our sins, that makes us brand
new, that washes our souls as clean and
pure as the day we were born, that gives
us the riches of the glory of Heaven, that
makes us heirs with Christ, and gives us
eternal life—that kind of love is found no-
where but in God.

Love is the first trait in the Fruit of
the Spirit because without love, none of
the other traits would be possible. This
love, this *Agape* love that transcends what
we know as love on earth is only known by
those who are loved by God through salvation in His Son, Jesus. It isn't something we
can buy, it is only available one way, and it
is worth more than any treasure.

Matthew 13:44-46 describes the
Kingdom of Heaven as a "great treasure"
and a "pearl of great price." In the parables here, the person who finds the treasure and the pearl sell everything they have
in order to obtain the objects of their desire. We don't have to sell everything to
have the treasures of Heaven, we just have
to accept Christ as our Savior and it is all
ours! The point of this parable is that when

we realize Christ is everything, accepting Him as Lord and Savior becomes the "great treasure", the "pearl of great price", and we realize we have absolutely everything we can think of and more than we can imagine or hope for, (Ephesians 3:20), including an everlasting and unending love.

We love God because He first loved us, (1 John 4:19). Romans 8:39 tells us nothing will separate us from the love of God. We can rest assured that when we are saved, we have the love of God in our lives. God will never leave nor forsake us (Hebrews 13:5). While it's possible for us to walk away from God, He will never walk away from us. There is no depths Jesus will not go to in order to pull us out of the muck and mire we get ourselves into.

This kind of love is called *Agape* love. It is the pure, unmerited love that Christ showed us by dying on the Cross for our sins. We do not deserve His love, we cannot earn His love, and we cannot stop His love no matter what we do. He is always willing to forgive us, no matter what. Luke 15:3-7 tells us that if even one sheep is lost, the shepherd will leave the others to search for the one that is lost. That is a

picture of Jesus and His love for us. We are
the lost sheep and He calls us to Himself.

No matter what your sin may be, or
how awful you think you are, there is nothing Christ is not willing to forgive you for if
you come to Him with a sincere heart and
ask. He already know what you've done,
you aren't going to shock or surprise Him.
So make the decision today to accept the
great and glorious love, the *Agape* love of
Jesus Christ.

~ * ~

Marie McGaha

Think about it!

Jesus Christ loves you more than anyone you've ever known ever could. He loves you so much He died for your sins so that you can have a relationship with Him. He loves you so much that He gave up Heaven to live as mortal man, to die a horrific death just so He can spend eternity with you! Don't let your pride or fear of the unknown keep you from your true destiny.

Pray!

Lord Jesus, Thank You for loving me beyond anything I've ever known. Thank You for dying on the Cross for me. I want to know you as my Lord and Savior. I want to spend my life serving You and living the life You planned for me before I was even born. I want to spend eternity in Heaven with You. Forgive me for my sins and help me to follow You and live my life right. In Jesus' Name. Amen.

Decide!

Do you know Jesus Christ as your Lord and Savior? What's stopping you? Is it fear? Pride? Don't let the devil rob you of a life fulfilled in Christ Jesus and don't let the devil take you to hell with him. If you aren't living for Heaven, then you are bound for hell. Choose this day whom you will serve (Joshua 24:15).

~ End ~

About the Author

Marie McGaha lives in Grangeville, Idaho with her husband, Nathan and a plethora of animals. She is the author of several Christian books, and writes sweet romance as Rie McGaha. She is an ordained minister, chaplain and teacher.

www.mariemcgaha.com

http://thelightofjesus.blogspot.com/

Follow her on

Facebook & Intstagram

Marie McGaha

Marie McGaha